Carlos Alcaraz

A Biography

Author: Alia Bouta

ALIAREDA © 2023

Information about Carlos Alcaraz

- ✔ The complete name is Carlos Alcaraz Garfia.

- ✔ Birth date: May 5 2003

- ✔ Place of birth: El Palmar, Murcia, Spain

- ✔ His ethnicity is Spanish

- ✔ Parents: Carlos Alvarez González (Spanish father) and Virginia Garfia Escandón (Spanish mother).

- ✔ lvaro, Sergio, and Jaime are sibs.

- ✔ For Alcaraz, Rafael Nadal is a popular tennis player.

- ✔ Year International Career 2018

- ✔ Occupational titles: six

- ✔ Right-handed backhand with two hands

- ✔ Prize money valued approximately 6.5 million dollars.

book plan

Introduction

Only a few professional tennis players have the ability to captivate fans and change the way the sport is played. Carlos Alcaraz is a young Spanish star who shines both on and off the court. This biography goes into great detail about Carlos Alcaraz's life and career. It shows how he went from being a very talented child to becoming one of the most exciting tennis players in recent years.

Join us as we go on an exciting and inspiring journey to find out how Carlos Alcaraz got to where he is today. His story is a mix of determination, perseverance, and an undying love for the game. Alcaraz's journey, from his humble beginnings in El Palmar, Spain, to his amazing success on the professional circuit, is sure to have a lasting effect on the tennis world.

Carlos Alcaraz has made a lot of money because he has won two Grand Slam tournaments. Before the US Open in 2022, he had made almost $6,300,000 USD in his career. When the tennis player won the Wimbledon championship in 2023 and got a prize of $3,1,000,000 USD, it was the first time that his income went over $20,000,000.

We get to know the person behind the tennis prodigy by learning about the less well-known parts of his personal life. We also learn about the struggles, sacrifices, and victories that have made him the great athlete he is today. As Alcaraz's star continues to rise, this biography shows how dedicated he is to his sport, how hard he works, and how he never stops trying to be the best. From his first steps into tennis to his big wins on the world stage, each chapter gives valuable information about the skills, mindset, and strategies that have helped Carlos Alcaraz reach the top of his game.

Get ready to see Carlos Alcaraz's amazing feats of perseverance, as well as some of the most exciting matches of his professional career. As we follow his path to success, we look at the delicate balance of talent and discipline that is needed to beat problems and become a tennis icon.

This biography isn't just a story about his career; it's also a story that shows how important it is to work hard and follow your dreams. Whether you're a big tennis fan or just like reading about interesting people, this biography will take you on an amazing journey through the life of one of tennis's most promising young players. Get ready for a fascinating look at ambition, grit, and the endless opportunities that lie ahead for those who dare to try to be great.

1. The Early Years of Carlos Alcaraz

Carlos Alcaraz was born on May 5, 2003, in a small town in Spain called El Palmar. El Palmar is in the Region of Murcia. From a very young age on, it was clear that Carlos loved tennis a lot. Since he was old enough to hold a racket, he's been seen swinging it with a level of determination that belies his age.

Carlos was lucky to grow up in a family that loved sports. His parents, José Antonio and Virginia, were always there to support and encourage him. They saw his talent and wanted to help him develop his love for the game. Carlos's father taught him how to play tennis when he was only three years old. He wanted Carlos to love tennis for the rest of his life.

When Carlos was young, he spent a lot of happy times on the tennis court. His father took him to the local tennis club every day, even when it was raining. There, Carlos started his training to become a professional tennis player.

Even though Carlos was too young to understand how the game worked at first, he went to every practice with a lot of enthusiasm. He would copy the moves and strokes of Rafael Nadal and Juan Martn del Potro, two tennis players he looked up to. Even though he was so young, he had an uncanny ability to play the same shots as the pros.

As Carlos got older, his parents decided he should take tennis lessons every week. He quickly got ahead of his peers, and his coaches were impressed by how talented and determined he was. Even though Carlos was the youngest player in his group, he often played against older kids and didn't back down from any challenge.

The local tennis community took notice of Carlos because of how hard he worked and how good he was. At the age of nine, he was asked to join the famous Juan Carlos Ferrero Equelite Sport Academy, which trains tennis players-to-be. This was a big turning point in his young career, as he was now surrounded by people who shared his interests and world-class coaches who helped him develop his skills and fuel his passion.

Carlos's parents were proud to see how their son took advantage of the opportunities at the academy. Even though he was away from home for long periods of time, he didn't give up and worked hard to make the most of his time there. When Carlos started winning a lot of junior tournaments, it was clear that his family had done the right thing.

It was clear that Carlos Alcaraz would go on to bigger and better things in tennis. He was destined for greatness because of how talented he was and how hard he worked. He had no idea that his childhood was just the start of an amazing journey that would see him rise through the ranks and become a major force in the world of tennis.

2. Detailed biography and career path

Carlos Alcaraz is a tennis player from Spain. His full name is Carlos Alcaraz Garfia. He was born in El Palmar, Spain, on May 5, 2003. Alcaraz is thought to be one of the best young tennis players in the world.

At the young age of four, Alcaraz began his tennis career, and his natural ability was evident right away. He trained a lot and played in many junior tournaments, where his skills and dedication to the sport made him stand out.

In 2018, when he was 15 years old, Alcaraz won the Junior Davis Cup for Spain. He helped his country win the tournament. This success was a big step forward for his young career.

On the ITF Futures tour in 2019, Alcaraz played his first match as a pro. In the same year, he won his first professional title, making him the youngest Spanish player ever to do so at age 16. He kept making a good impression in 2020, when he won more titles on the ITF Futures tour.

In 2021, Alcaraz made headlines when he won the Australian Open for the first time. In the second round, he beat an experienced player, David Goffin, and became the youngest player since 1992 to win a main draw match at a Grand Slam. This win put him in the spotlight around the world and showed how much he could do.

It's no secret that Alcaraz plays with an aggressive mentality and powerful groundstrokes. Many experts and fans compare his game to that of Rafael Nadal, who is also from Spain.

Alcaraz was ranked #38 in the world by the ATP in singles as of September 2021. This was his best ranking ever. Already at the age of 18, he is one of the sport's brightest young stars. Fans all over the world are excited to see what he does next.

Carlos Alcaraz is a tennis player from Spain who makes a living at it. He was born in Murcia, Spain, on May 5, 2003. Alcaraz loved tennis from a very young age. He started playing when he was only three years old.

Carlos Sr. and Aranzazu Alcaraz were big fans of their son's tennis career and saw his talent when he was young. They put him in tennis academies and made sure he got the coaching and training he needed to get better.

Alcaraz's childhood was all about tennis, and he spent a lot of time practicing and getting better at it. At age 15, he quit school to try to make a living as a professional tennis player. This choice was made so that he could focus on training and compete in international tournaments.

Alcaraz's early career was marked by extraordinary talent and a distinctive style of play. His game is strong and aggressive, and he is known for his strong groundstrokes and amazing athleticism. His natural skills and his commitment to training helped him move up through the junior tennis ranks.

Alcaraz won the Junior Australian Open in 2019, making him the first Spanish player to do so since Rafael Nadal. This win put him at the top of the junior rankings and made people in the tennis world take notice.

Professional tennis players and experts took notice of Alcaraz's success as a young player. He is seen by many as one of the most promising young athletes. In 2020, he played in the main draw of the Rio Open for the first time. He became the fourth-youngest player to win an ATP Tour match.

Today, Carlos Alcaraz is still making progress in his career, and the ATP ranks him as one of the top 100 players. Even though he is young, he has a level of maturity and calmness on the court that makes him stand out from other players his age.

Carlos Alcaraz's childhood and first experiences with tennis were important parts of how he became a tennis player. His hard work, skill, and love for tennis have made him a rising star in the world of tennis, and fans can't wait to see what the future holds for this young Spanish star.

His sudden rise up the World Rankings hasn't been talked about much until now. After his US Open victory in 2022, Alcaraz rocketed into the top 50 in the world from outside the top 100 in 2021. The Spanish tennis player was ranked eleventh in the world after he won in Miami. Alcaraz kept his winning streak going at the Barcelona Open, and at the Madrid Open, he set a new record. Caracarz shocked the tennis world when he beat Nadal and Djokovic on back-to-back days. He was the last player to do this in one match. It's impressive that he beat Alexander Zverev in his last match. Alcaraz had the chance to become famous all over the world.

He also has a flat, deep backhand that he can use to hit line drives out of the park. His opponents are pushed back into the court by his powerful groundstrokes, and he follows them up with crucial drop shots that are often too well-placed and hidden for him to control. At crucial points in the match, he frequently employs the serve-volley in addition to his strong groundstrokes and deadly volleys. Carlos Alcaraz is a tennis player who can play in many different positions. His favorite way to play is aggressively from the baseline, which helps him win more points with his forehand. He can either add height and reach from beyond the baseline or make a quick, flat shot that lets him win from anywhere on the court.

Alcaraz trains at the Juan Carlos Ferrero Equelite Sport Academy in Villena, Spain, and at the Rafa Nadal Academy in Manacor, Spain. Young tennis players who want to improve their skills and reach their full potential can get the best training and coaching at these academies. After winning the French Open in 2003, Ferrero realized that he was playing against the best tennis players in history, like Roger Federer. From 2019 to 2022, he made Carlos Alcaraz a worldwide star by getting him to win the last US Open and become the best player in the world.

At the Australian Open, Alcaraz was the youngest player in the men's singles draw. He was only seventeen. He won his first match but lost his second. On the national level, the Spaniard was the youngest winner in the history of the Madrid Open.

Alcaraz knew a lot at a young age because he had learned a lot. He first played on the ATP Tour at the Rio Open in February 2020. Before that, he had played in Challengers. He was still getting good results after a year.

The Juan Carlos Ferrero Equelite Sport Academy was started by the former No. 1 tennis player in the world, Juan Carlos Ferrero. Its goal is to give young players a full training program. The academy focuses on the technical, tactical, physical, and mental aspects of the game and offers personalized training plans to meet each player's needs.

On the other hand, Rafael Nadal, a famous tennis player from Spain, set up the Rafa Nadal Academy.

Young tennis players can learn both how to play tennis and how to do well in school at the academy. They offer a structured program that combines intense training on the court with schoolwork so that students can keep going to school while pursuing tennis careers.

No thought was given to where the first shot was fired in the transmission, but it was fired at about 210 km/h. Because of this, its effectiveness was called into question. This meant that people didn't like his service either. Clients don't like what he does. The second effect, on the other hand, is always there and is the best. The ball can be deflected by a high bounce on the field, and a topspin can make a close opponent's return weak. Most of the time, she does her second climb between

150 and 170 km/h. Carlos Alcaraz has the same problem as other rookies: he serves the ball with too much force when it needs to be more delicate, and he often makes mistakes that lead to fouls. On the other hand, he works hard and grows by actively trying to talk to people at base and only getting more aggressive when he has a good chance to hit. Carlos Alcaraz is well-known for how well he has done in sports. People have compared him to tennis greats like Rafael Nadal and Gael Monfils because of how fast he is and how well he can play from tight spots. His strong doubling and gliding around the court on defense, especially on the backhand, where he can counter his opponent's aggression on groundstrokes or drop shots, have led to comparisons to Novak Djokovic in terms of mobility and coverage of the court. People have compared

him to Roger Federer because of how well he moves on his feet, how strong his forehand is, and how he can control the game. Since he was young, his mental strength and endurance have impressed people. This led Martina Navrátilová, John McEnroe, and Mark Petchey, among others, to say that he would one day be world No. 1 and win many Grand Slam titles.

Carlos Alcaraz's quick rise in tennis is likely due to the fact that he trained at these academies. He has been able to get help from experienced coaches and use top-notch facilities to improve his skills and game. Carlos Alcaraz is one of the most promising young Spanish tennis players because he is talented, works hard, and gets help from these academies.

Carlos Alcaraz had to drop out of the 2023 Australian Open because he hurt his right leg. His exercise had hurt a muscle in his hamstrings called the semimembranosus. A few weeks later, he won the competition back in Buenos Aires, but he lost twice to Cameron Norrie in Rio de Janeiro. During the race, he hurt his thigh again.

Alcaraz is always compared to Rafael Nadal, another great Spaniard who plays well on clay, and this is often done in a mean way. Even though Alcaraz and Nadal are both strong, confident athletes, their styles of play couldn't be more different. The main difference between Alcaraz and Nadal is that Alcaraz is right-handed and Nadal is left-handed. In Rio de Janeiro in 2020, he was 16 when he won his first match on the

ATP Tour. He was 17 when he broke into the top 100, and he was 18 when he won his first ATP Tour title.

The Equelite Sport Academy is a tennis school run by Carlos Alcaraz and Carlos Ferrero. It is in Villena, Spain. Former professional tennis player Carlos Ferrero started the academy. In 2003, when he was at the top of his game, he was ranked world no. 1.

The academy helps young people who want to play tennis improve their skills, techniques, and mental strength through training and coaching. It has a wide range of programs and training options for players of all skill levels, from beginners to experts and professionals.

A young tennis player from Spain named Carlos Alcaraz has trained at the academy. He is thought to be one of the tennis world's rising stars because of his talent and potential.

Carlos Alcaraz and other young tennis players get a complete tennis education at the academy. This includes technical training, physical conditioning, mental preparation, and experience playing in tournaments. The academy wants to help players grow in all ways, not just in terms of tennis skills, but also in terms of character development and personal growth. Carlos Alcaraz and Carlos Ferrero Equelite Sport Academy has a reputation for turning out good tennis players. Some of its graduates have gone on to play at the highest level of professional tennis. The academy keeps getting young athletes from all over the world because it gives them the tools and help, they need to reach their full potential in the sport.

Even though Alcaraz lost to Novak Djokovic, the good news is that he is once again the best player in the world. Since Rafael Nadal won in Miami and Madrid in 2005, the 19-year-old Spaniard is the youngest player to win three straight Masters 1000 titles. The city will have four if you count Madrid 2023. After a break in March 2023, Because of a thigh injury he got in Rio de Janeiro, Alcaraz won at Indian Wells and has now won five straight matches. Carlos got into a rhythm quickly and showed off his skills by beating Daniil Medvedev in straight sets. Medvedev had won 19 titles before, including three in a row.

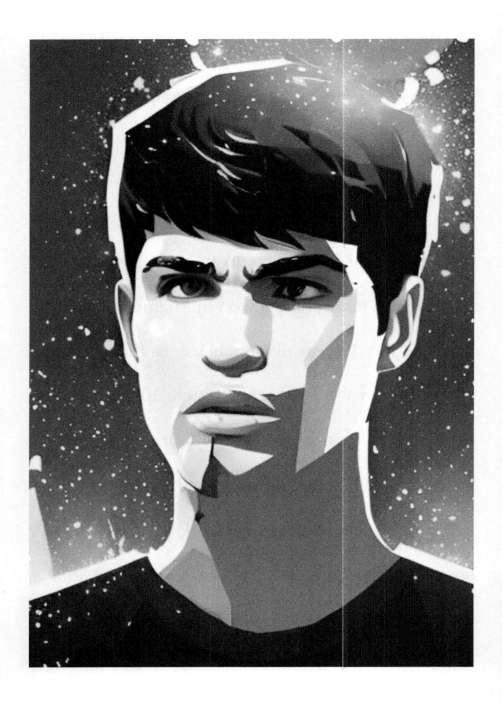

In the second round of Wimbledon on grass, the number two player in the world, Daniil Medvedev, beat Alcaraz. He beat the Serb Filip Krajinovi, the Spanish Albert Ramos-Vinolas, and the Frenchman Richard Gasquet to win his first ATP title in Umag at the end of July. In October, he beat former world number one Daniel Evans, Britain's Andy Murray, and Italy's Matteo Berrettini to get to the semifinals of an indoor tournament in Vienna. The match took 2 hours and 40 minutes. Alexander Zverev, a German, beat him. Zverev won in 1 hour and 8 minutes. At the Paris-Bercy Masters, he beat Pierre-Hugues Herbert and Jannik Sinner to get to the round of 16. Even though he was up 5:0 against Hugo Gaston, a French qualifier, he lost the Davis Cup match.

In Winston-Salem, he tried hard, but the Swiss player Mikael Ymer beat him. After that, he beat British No. 26 Cameron Norrie in three sets to win the US Open. But he loses one set to the Frenchman Arthur Rinderknech. However, he beats the world number three, the Greek Stéfanos Tsitsipás, in a third-round match that lasts more than four hours and lets him move on to the second week. He is the youngest player since the American Michael Chang in 1989 to beat one of the top three players in the world. After three and a half hours of play, he beat Peter Gojowczyk of Germany, who was not very good, to stay in the tournament. The Canadian Felix Auger-Aliassime had to leave the second round because he was having pain in his right shoulder.

Alcaraz's technical skills were developed at a young age because he is easy to train and has the natural ability to copy movements and understand any kind of information. During his teen years, he went through a lot of high-quality training. The goal was to help him do a better job. At first, Alcaraz had trouble because of his size and strength. Alcaraz had to talk to Juanjo Lopez, an expert on growth, to figure out how to solve his big problem. Alcaraz had to spend more time playing tennis if he wanted to get stronger. Alcaraz's speed and stamina got better when he competed against older, more experienced athletes.

In 2021, he beat David Goffin of Belgium to win the Great Ocean Road Open, but he lost in the qualifying round of the Australian Open to Botic van de

Zandschultz. Carlos Alcaraz won all of his matches at the Next Generation ATP Finals. He only lost one set to Juan Manuel Cerndolo of Argentina, and in the finals, he beat Sebastian Korda in 1 hour and 20 minutes.

The Rafa Nadal Academy is a tennis school in the Spanish city of Manacor, on the island of Mallorca. It was started in 2016 by Rafael Nadal, a tennis player from Spain, and his family. The goal of the academy is to give young tennis players the chance to learn and train with the same ideas and methods that have made Nadal one of the best tennis players of all time.

The Rafa Nadal Academy has helped many promising players, like Carlos Alcaraz, improve their skills and reach their goals in the sport.

Carlos Alcaraz's unique and mysterious style of play has shaken up the tennis world. He gives the sport a new look by combining power, agility, and skill in a way that keeps people around the world watching. In this chapter, we'll look at the different parts of Alcaraz's game and try to figure out what makes him so good on the court.

Alcaraz's groundstrokes are one of the things that make him stand out as a player. He can control the game from the baseline because he has a fierce forehand and a backhand that can generate a lot of speed.

Alcaraz's skill lets him get to the ball early and hit it with great timing and accuracy. His groundstrokes are so strong that his opponents often have to scramble to get back at him.

Alcaraz became only the second player after Rafael Nadal (2012, 2013) to win back-to-back titles in Madrid. He did this by beating Alexander Zverev (2022) and Jan-Lennard Struff (2023). The 2022 championship was the most important because it was the end of a great season. "Carlitos" made history when he beat Rafael Nadal in the quarterfinals, Novak Djokovic in the semifinals, and Alexander Zverev in the final. He was the first person to beat both Nadal and the Spaniard in the same clay event. Without Djokovic and Nadal in 2023, it was clear that Alcaraz was the favorite. When he was younger, he won his first title in Barcelona. Since 2021, he hasn't lost, and his winning streak keeps going in Madrid. In the second round of the Rome tournament, the Hungarian player Fabian Marozsan beat him and sent him home.

Alcaraz is not happy to just hit groundstrokes back and forth from the baseline. He plays in a way that makes him stand out: he is aggressive. He is good at attacking when he sees a chance, and he always tries to win when he can. His aggressive shots often catch his opponents off guard because he goes for big winners without fear, both down the line and across the court.

For such a young player, Alcaraz has a lot of speed and agility on the court. He has great footwork, which lets him move quickly and get balls that seem impossible to get. Alcaraz's defensive skills are very good, and it's especially impressive how well he can predict his opponent's shots. Together with his quick reflexes, this lets him stop opponents who are being too aggressive and turn defense into offense.

Recent wins on clay courts at the 500 level in Rio de Janeiro in February 2022 and at the US Open in September 2021 show how fast he is. After winning the US Open in September 2022, Carlos Alcaraz became the youngest player ever to be at the top of the ATP rankings. These rankings have been kept since 1973. Leyton Hewitt held the record before. He was 20 years old when he first reached the top of the rankings in 2001.

Alcaraz is mostly known for his skills at the baseline, but he also has a lot of impressive skills at the net. He has great touch and accuracy in his volleys and drop shots, which often catch his opponents by surprise. Alcaraz approaches the net with confidence and intelligence whenever he has a chance to finish off points with style and grace.

Alcaraz's unquestionable mental strength and resilience are also important parts of his game. Even when there is a lot of pressure on him, he stays calm and makes good decisions. Even when the game is close, Alcaraz doesn't hesitate to take shots. This shows that he has a mature and focused mind.

Carlos Alcaraz's tennis style is a tempting mix of power, speed, aggression, and skill. He has a unique set of skills that allow him to be the best player from the baseline and also show how good he is at the net. Even though he is young, Alcaraz is a tough opponent because of how strong-minded and determined he is. As he continues to make waves in the tennis world, we can't wait to see how his mysterious style of play changes and grows.

Carlos Alcaraz is the next big thing in Spanish tennis, and he has had a very exciting start to his career. Even though he is only 18, he has already gained attention from all over the world because of how well he plays and how hard he works on the court. Alcaraz has been a professional athlete for a short time, but he has already won a lot of trophies. Each one is a big step forward in his career.

Carlos Alcaraz got his first big tennis recognition when he was given a wild card into the Australian Open in 2020. He was only 16 years old at the time. Even though he didn't win the main prize, this trophy showed his potential and reminded him of the chances he still had.

In 2020, Carlos Alcaraz led the Spanish team to win the Junior Davis Cup, which showed how hard he worked and how good he was. With his amazing play throughout the tournament, he helped Spain win the tournament's top prize and earn a place in history.

At the Trieste Open in Italy in August 2020, Alcaraz won his first ATP Challenger title. The moment of victory was his big break because he beat skilled professionals and proved he could do well at the senior level. This trophy was the first step on his way to becoming one of the best tennis players in the world.

In March 2021, Carlos Alcaraz won again at the ATP Challenger in Barcelona, which showed that he was still getting better. This victory showed how hard he worked and how talented he was. He solidified his reputation as a rising star in the tennis world by keeping his cool throughout the tournament.

In July 2021, Carlos Alcaraz made history by becoming the youngest Spaniard in more than 20 years to win an ATP title. In an exciting final, he beat Richard Gasquet to win the Umag Open in Croatia. The fact that he won his first ATP title at age 18 showed that he had a lot of potential and made him one of the most promising young players.

Carlos Alcaraz got a wild card into the US Open, and his great performance there shocked both fans and experts. For the first time, he made it to the fourth round of a Grand Slam. Along the way, he beat well-known players like Stefanos Tsitsipas. Even though he didn't make it to the quarterfinals, his amazing run showed off his amazing skills and won him the respect of the tennis world.

Carlos Alcaraz was a young man with a lot of talent. He won awards in every international category for young people. In 2017, he won the singles title at the U16 European Championships. In 2018, he won the Davis Cup for Juniors with Spain.

Carlos Alcaraz continues to amaze tennis fans all over the world with his amazing skills, unwavering drive, and trophy case that shows how quickly he has risen in the professional ranks. Every time he wins, he adds a new chapter to his already amazing story. This shows that he is going to be a great tennis player.

When he was four years old, Carlos Alcaraz played tennis at Real Sociedad Club de Campo de Murcia. Because his father wanted his son to be taught by reliable people, he first chose Carlos Santos Bosque and then Kiko Navarro. Navarro says that Alcaraz played for the first time when he was four years old. While they played, he showed his father all the amazing things he could do. Children this age often have trouble returning a simple ball. He was having a fight with his dad. It was great how everything turned out. Since it was started in a small town of 24,000 people near Murcia in southeast Spain, Alcaraz has been gaining more and more supporters. Carlos Santos Bosque was the first person to train Alcaraz. Three young men his age, Pedro, Fulgencio, and Javi, visit him at the facility twice a week. The group has a large number of fans. In the near future, they will be able to get training that is more interesting and more often.

Alcaraz won his first match in a Challenger event in Alicante when he was 15 years old. He is now trained by Juan Carlos Ferrero. As a junior in Villena at the same school, he played in Grade 1 and made it to the quarterfinals of Wimbledon. Then, in Dénia, he won his first professional game.

The goal was to become the second-best player in Spain who was not a professional. The family didn't have enough money for any of them to go to the Bruguera Academy in Barcelona. He was named director of the organization in the end. Santos Bosque is one of the newest people to live there. Before Santos Bosque taught Kiko Navarro how to train Carlitos, Kiko Navarro was in charge of Carlitos. But Carlos Alcaraz's father didn't think he knew enough to teach his son on his own, so he gave him to a reliable person. That person will be Navarro. Carlos Alcaraz Sr. will be in charge of making sure that Carlos Alcaraz Jr. grows up safely and wisely.

He lives with fellow tennis player Maria Gonzalez Gimenez, who won the US Open in September. It looks like they met at the Murcia Tennis Club in Murcia, Spain, where they both played tennis. Some of the champion's family members say that the two of them have been friends since they were young. Still, the 23-year-old would rather keep to herself. The couple doesn't post pictures of each other on social networking sites very often. Even on the tennis court, she doesn't get as close to her partner as she could.

Over the course of their careers, Rafael Nadal, Roger Federer, and Novak Djokovic have all changed how they play tennis in order to do well. Carlos Alcaraz, who is twenty years old, seems to have a deep understanding of the court, which sometimes reaches extreme heights. We are very unlikely to have ever met anyone like him. It moves just as quickly as Rafa Nadal. It has a strong Defense, a strong Right, and a strong Right. Recently, Kei Nishikori, who will be back on the tennis courts this week, said that having to play against him for a few more years would keep him motivated. The "Big 3" is made up of the three most well-known sports champions until July 2023. Last year, Carlos Alcaraz was often compared to them in a good way, and many people think he has their skills. But Patrick Mouratoglou doesn't want to talk about the "Big Three" of Spanish music. Most of the time, when we say "Big 3," we mean Roger, Rafa, and Novak, who have won more than 20 world titles between them.

Alcaraz's technical skills started when he was young because he was a player who was easy to train and was naturally good at copying movements and understanding any kind of information. As a child, he went to a lot of high-quality training sessions. His work would be better because of the instruction. At first, Alcaraz's biggest problems were his height and his ability to keep going. Alcaraz had to talk to Juanjo Lopez, an expert on growth, about his problem with his height. Alcaraz had to spend more time playing tennis so that he could get stronger. Alcaraz's performance and stamina got better because he could talk to people older than him.

3. Carlos Alcaraz and Rafael Nadal

Over the years, many young tennis players have become stars, and Carlos Alcaraz's rise in recent years has made people compare him to the legendary Rafael Nadal. This chapter looks at how these two Spanish tennis stars are alike and how they are different. It focuses on their playing styles, career accomplishments, and effects on the sport.

On the court, both Alcaraz and Nadal are very strong and play with a lot of intensity. Alcaraz is often compared to a young Nadal because of his powerful groundstrokes and aggressive baseline play. In the same way, Nadal's game is based on his great footwork, topspin forehand with his left hand, and relentless defense, which have become his trademarks.

Rafael Nadal is considered to be one of the best tennis players ever. Nadal is the best player on clay courts. He has won 20 Grand Slam titles, including a record 13 French Opens. Alcaraz, on the other hand, is still early in his career, but he has already reached important points. In 2021, he got to the quarterfinals of his first Grand Slam tournament, the US Open. He was the youngest man to get that far since 1963. This bold start shows that he has the ability to match or even beat some of Nadal's achievements.

One important thing that Alcaraz and Nadal have in common is that they both respect and like each other. Alcaraz has said many times that he looks up to and gets ideas from Nadal. Nadal, on the other hand, has praised Alcaraz's talent and said that the young player will do well in the future. The way Nadal helped and influenced Alcaraz is a good example of how legendary players can help the next generation.

Both players are very competitive on the court, but they act and act like different people. Nadal is known for being a good sport, being humble, and treating his opponents with respect. He has a reputation for being fair and kind, which has earned him the respect of fans all over the world. Alcaraz is still growing as a player, but he is often called fiery and passionate, and he sometimes loses his cool during games. This shows how different their levels of maturity and stages of development are.

The quick rise of Carlos Alcaraz, which reminds people of the early years of Rafael Nadal, has led to comparisons between the two Spanish tennis stars. Even though their playing styles are similar, comparing the chapters shows that Nadal is well on his way to becoming a legend, while Alcaraz is just starting to make a name for himself. Time will tell if Alcaraz can live up to his countryman's high expectations, but his talent, drive, and Nadal's help make him an exciting prospect for the future of tennis.

4. Carlos Alcaraz vs Roger Federer

Carlos Alcaraz is a rising star in the world of tennis. His impressive wins and exciting style of play have been making a lot of noise. In this chapter, we'll look at how Alcaraz and the legendary Roger Federer are alike and different. We'll focus on their playing styles, career paths, and effects on the sport of tennis.

Carlos Alcaraz and Roger Federer are both known for playing in an elegant and stylish way. Even though Alcaraz is young, he has a great sense of control, accuracy, and making shots with force. He has a strong forehand and a good game all over the court. In the same way, Federer's game is known for his perfect technique, fluidity, and graceful footwork. He is known for his versatility and ability to make different kinds of shots, such as his famous one-handed backhand.

Carlos Alcaraz is still early in his career, but he has already reached a few important points. He joined the ATP when he was 16 years old and became the youngest player since Rafael Nadal in 2004 to reach the semifinals of an ATP 250 event. On the other hand, Roger Federer has had a brilliant career that has lasted more than 20 years. Federer has won a record 20 Grand Slam titles and was ranked No. 1 in the world for a record 310 weeks. He is one of the best tennis players of all time because he has played for so long and won so often.

Carlos Alcaraz has quickly become known for his promising tennis skills. Because he is Spanish and plays like Rafael Nadal, he is often compared to Nadal. Alcaraz has already gotten the attention of tennis fans all over the world, and his quick rise has made people excited and curious about how far he could go in the future. Roger Federer, on the other hand, has done more for tennis than anyone else. Federer is seen by many as a global icon, and he has done a lot to make tennis popular around the world. Fans of all ages have loved him for his style, sportsmanship, and charisma.

Even though Carlos Alcaraz is still early in his career and hasn't had as much success as Roger Federer yet, they both have an elegant way of playing tennis and have made an impact on the sport. Alcaraz's talent and performance so far show that he has a bright future ahead of him, while Federer's legendary career will always be a model for future players to follow. It will be interesting to watch Alcaraz's journey and see if he can find his own way and possibly reach the same heights in tennis as Federer.

5. Carlos Alcaraz vs Novak Djokovic

In the exciting and fast-paced world of professional tennis, there are legends who have left an indelible mark on the sport. Novak Djokovic, a tennis superstar from Serbia, and Carlos Alcaraz, a tennis prodigy from Spain, stand out as two tennis players who have wowed fans all over the world. In this chapter, we compare these two great athletes in depth, looking at their backgrounds, playing styles, and accomplishments.

Novak Djokovic first became known as a tennis player in the early 2000s. In 2003, he started his professional career. Djokovic is from Belgrade, Serbia. He had a lot of talent from a young age and was quickly seen as a future sports star. He is now one of the "Big Three" men's tennis players, along with Roger Federer and Rafael Nadal. Together, they have broken many records and won many titles.

On the other hand, Carlos Alcaraz is a rising tennis star. Alcaraz was born in Murcia, Spain, in 2003. From a young age, he showed how talented he was. He started playing on the ATP Tour in 2019, when he was only sixteen years old. He impressed tennis fans with his fierce determination and impressive skills. Alcaraz is seen as one of the most promising young athletes, and he has been compared to players like Nadal and Djokovic.

Djokovic is known for his great defense and ability to

return any shot better than anyone else. Because he is so flexible and quick on the court, he can reach balls that seem almost impossible to return. Djokovic frustrates his opponents by always getting the ball back into play. He does this with his great footwork and incredible ability to think ahead. Also, his strong backhand and accurate shots have given him an edge over most of his competitors.

6. The Rise of Carlos Alcaraz Tennis Business

But Carlos's athletic success is not the only way he makes money. Firman also has contracts with well-known companies to advertise for them. Nike gives him clothes and shoes to wear. In January 2022, a contract for sponsorship was finalized with the high-end watch brand Rolex. Uses tennis racquets made by Babolat, a French company.

Young and talented tennis player Carlos Alcaraz has taken the world by storm with his skills and drive. But his rising popularity isn't just due to how well he does on the court. In fact, Alcaraz has also tried his hand at business. He started a successful tennis-related business that has caught the attention of both fans and experts in the field. This chapter looks at how Carlos Alcaraz built his tennis business empire and how it has helped him be successful in general.

As Carlos Alcaraz's tennis career took off, he realized that he could leave a legacy that went beyond his wins on the court. He saw a chance to build a name for himself that would go beyond his own accomplishments and have a lasting effect on the sport he loved. With this goal in mind, Alcaraz set out to build his own tennis business empire around his unique style of play and dedication to the game.

Alcaraz put together a team of experts who knew how the tennis business worked so they could help him get his business off the ground. He worked with marketing strategists and business managers who had a lot of experience and helped him build a solid foundation for his business. Together, they made a business plan that covered many different parts of the world of tennis.

The Carlos Alcaraz Tennis Academy was one of the most important things that Carlos Alcaraz did. The academy was in El Palmar, Spain, where he grew up. Its goal was to help young tennis players develop their skills and give them the tools they needed to succeed in the tough world of tennis. Here, Alcaraz worked closely with a team of experienced coaches who shared his love of tennis and helped shape the next generation of players.

Carlos Alcaraz also tried his hand at fashion by starting his own clothing line. The line was full of trendy and useful clothes for tennis players that showed off his unique style and personality. Alcaraz quickly gained a loyal following of fans who wanted to look like him on the court by using his wide fame and admiration for the way he played.

As Alcaraz's skill and popularity kept growing, so did the chances for him to get endorsements. He carefully chose partnerships with well-known sports brands that fit with the goals and values of his brand. Through these partnerships, Alcaraz not only got lucrative endorsement deals, but he also got to represent brands that shared his love of tennis and sportsmanship.

Carlos Alcaraz thought it was very important to give back to his community and help good causes. Through his tennis business, he set up the Carlos Alcaraz Foundation, a non-profit group whose goal is to get tennis into the lives of poor kids and help them become more independent through the sport. The foundation made sure that every aspiring tennis player had the same chance to follow their dreams by giving them scholarships, equipment, and access to training facilities.

Carlos Alcaraz's move into business shows how entrepreneurial he is and how much he wants to leave behind a lasting legacy. Carlos Alcaraz has built a tennis business empire. He has a tennis academy, a clothing line, and endorsement deals. All of these things add to his stellar tennis career and give him the chance to inspire and help other tennis players. Alcaraz continues to break down barriers and prove that he is a true game-changer both on and off the court through his business ventures.

7. Key factors for success and Key factors for failure for Carlos Alcaraz

Key factors for success for Carlos Alcaraz may include:

1. Extraordinary Talent: As a tennis player, Carlos Alcaraz has extraordinary talent and skills. He has shown a lot of promise at a young age and can compete at the highest level.

2.Hard Work and Dedication: Alcaraz's success can be credited to the fact that he worked hard and was dedicated to his craft. He is known for the hard work he puts into training and practicing, which has helped him improve his game and become successful.

3. Mental Strength: Alcaraz has shown mental toughness and resilience on the court, which has helped him do well under pressure and deal with problems. His success is largely due to the fact that he can stay focused and calm in tough situations.

4. Coaching and support: Alcaraz has benefited from a strong support system, which includes coaching and advice from professionals with a lot of experience. This help has helped him improve his game and make the changes he needed to make to be successful.

Key factors for failure for Carlos Alcaraz may include:

1. Injuries: Injuries can make it hard for a player to play well and make progress. If Alcaraz keeps getting

hurt and needs to rest for a long time or can't play as well, it could set him back and even cause him to fail.

2. Not being consistent: Being consistent is very important if you want to have a successful tennis career. If Alcaraz can't keep up a consistent level of play or his performance goes up and down, it could slow his progress and cause him to fail.

3. Mental and emotional challenges: Tennis is a sport that requires a lot of thinking, and if Alcaraz has trouble dealing with pressure, it could hurt his performance and his confidence. Mental and emotional problems can slow him down and even cause him to fail.

4. Tough Competition: The world of professional tennis is very competitive, and playing against tough opponents often can be hard. If Alcaraz always has trouble with top-ranked players or can't adjust to different ways of playing, it could slow his progress and cause him to fail.

8. The Passion for Hobbies: Carlos Alcaraz's Love for Tennis

Carlos Alcaraz is the next big thing in tennis. His amazing skills and relentless drive on the court have wowed crowds. But, like any successful athlete, Carlos knows that life needs to be balanced. In this chapter, we talk about Carlos Alcaraz's hobbies and interests, which fuel his love of tennis and help him grow as a person.

Carlos Alcaraz has been interested in tennis since he was a child. As a child growing up in the small Spanish town of El Palmar, Carlos would often go with his parents to a nearby tennis club. There, he would watch players of all ages and get ideas from their strong shots and smooth footwork. This first experience got

Carlos interested and set him on the path to improve his own skills.

From the first time Carlos picked up a tennis racket, he had a strong desire to be the best. He spent a lot of time perfecting his technique and fitness as part of his training routine, which became an important part of his daily life. Carlos's love for tennis kept him going through challenges and setbacks, which helped him reach the top of the professional tennis world.

Even though tennis is a big part of Carlos Alcaraz's life, he knows it's important to have other interests as well. Carlos does a lot of different things when he's not playing tennis. These things help him relax, unwind, and get ideas. One of his favorite things to do is play the guitar, which lets him show off his creative side and relax through music.

Carlos Alcaraz has also found that he loves taking pictures. Through his camera, Carlos captures the beauty of his surroundings, whether it's breathtaking landscapes or natural moments with his family and friends. Carlos uses photography to express his artistic side and appreciate the beauty of the world. It gives him a break from the stress of professional sports.

Carlos Alcaraz finds peace and comfort in nature, and he often goes outside to re-energize his mind and body. Hiking, riding a bike, and seeing new places gives him a sense of freedom and a new point of view that go beyond the tennis court. These trips outside feed his soul and give him a much-needed break from his busy sports career.

Carlos Alcaraz is always committed to tennis, but his interests go far beyond the court. Carlos gets ideas, creativity, and a sense of peace from his hobbies, such as playing the guitar, getting into photography, and exploring the great outdoors. These hobbies not only help him grow as a person, but they also improve his tennis skills. This shows that a well-rounded life improves his performance in all areas.

Conclusion

The story of how a young tennis prodigy beat all odds to become a rising star in the world of tennis is told in Carlos Alcaraz's biography. From his humble beginnings in Spain to his meteoric rise through the ranks, Alcaraz's incredible determination, unwavering perseverance, and amazing talent shine through, leaving an indelible mark on the sport.

Through the pages of this book, readers can see how hard Alcaraz worked to be successful, how hungry he was to get better, and how much he loved the game. This biography not only tells the whole story of Alcaraz's personal and professional life, but it also goes into the struggles, victories, and sacrifices he made behind the scenes that made him the tennis star he is today. Carlos Alcaraz's story shows aspiring athletes that anything is possible if they work hard, believe in themselves, and have passion for what they do.